How to Speak English Fast
Published by 12 Streams Publishing
June 12, 2018
Photocopial for student use only!
Consent is not given for reprinting or reproduction
ISBN : 978-0-9982006-7-5
Contact info@12secs.com for ordering

12 Secs.com

BY PROFESSOR TAMILLA PALMER PERERA
KOREAN CONTRIBUTED BY KWANGJUN CHOI
ASELA PERERA, EDITING ASST.

3

4

Table of Contents

Table of Contents (Cont'd)

AUTHOR'S Note – This book is designed to be a quick and strong introduction to the English language for new students of English. It only includes a few English rules and heavily leans to English verbs because these simple verbs are so valuable to a new student. In fact, this is the way in which the author taught herself how to speak Chinese. These lessons are not comprehensive nor do they cover the many topics for fluency such as grammar and paragraph reading.

Having taught English as a Second Language for 20 years, the author believes beginner students who are given paragraphs to read are immediately stunted because the amount of material which must be translated/comprehended is insurmountable. Short and concise, relative sentences are powerful!

This system, Champion English, so named because students feel empowered by being able to master small tidbits of information, has simply proven to be highly effective when taught in classrooms of over 23 nations and produced results in as few as two weeks. It is in line with the Common Core Standards that beginner "emerging" students must learn "many verbs and many verb tenses" in order to learn how English works see CA CCSS for ELA/Literacy RL.1.5; W.1.1-3; SL 1.4.

Photocopial with limitations. This book may be reproduced for student usage only for a single class. It is not to be reprinted. Also, if multiple locations are involved, a new text must be purchased for each location. By choosing to use this book, users assume complete responsibility for their learning and take complete responsibility for their actions.

Professor Tamilla Palmer Perera became an English expert at Nanchang University in Jiangxi, China in 2001. She has taught English language learners for over 25 years from ages 1-70 from the U.S., China, Hong Kong, Singapore, Brazil, Japan, Korea, Vietnam, Sri Lanka, France, Russia and numerous other places including Aspect International, Kaplan, GEOS, ELS, Language Systems, Whittier College, Citrus College, Sylvan Learning and school districts throughout Southern California. She lives in Los Angeles, California, is married to Asela Perera, graduated from University of Southern California (USC), and holds a master's equivalency in TESOL. She is affectionately known as "Mrs. Pea" on the public school campuses, Tamilla in private schools and Professor Palmer Perera among distinguished schools where she has led courses for as many as 350 university students per semester..

Teacher's Guide & Recommendations

1. These lessons are intended for a 55-minute class of students assessed as Beginner English, lowest level.
2. Give the directions in English. Teachers can point to the directions for the appropriate student's language.
3. Allow students to use dictionaries/translators to look up the words for the new vocabulary and homework only.
4. Pacing: Students should take no more than 2 days per Chapter. In order to provide the needed foundation to catch-up on the entire class lessons, they *MUST* do homework and work through this workbook quickly.
5. Give a quiz daily. Use any of the lessons as quiz material. Help students reach for the stars!

Learning Outcomes Relative to Common Core California Standards		Expanded activities not included in lesson
Listening Actively SL.K.1-10	Translation/Acquisition - Learn New Vocabulary Students will be able to translate a new word into English.	Students write a synonym in English or the definition of the word
Evaluating How well students speak RL.K.1-10	Replication – Write it 3 times Students will be able to write in English and to recollect how to use blends and phonics	Students can practice saying the word out loud one student at a time and or with a partner
Reading and Viewing Closely R.L.1-10	Detection - Guess the Word Students will be able to practice recall and word recognition	Students can guess other words hidden in the letters for extra points.
Using Verbs W.K. 5-10	Conjugation – Conjugate Students will practice subject verb agreement	Students read out loud as a class, I go, You go, He goes, She goes, We go, They go. Discuss /es/ with double consonants
Understanding Text Structure W.K. 4-10	Verb identification -Underline the verbs Students will be able to use grammar skills and distinct noun and verbs	Look up the verb in an English dictionary. Find synonyms
Composing and Writing Text and Presenting and Explaining Information W.K. 1-10	Duplication - Copy the sentence Students will be able to use capitalization, punctuation and sentence structure	Students can read the sentence out loud to partner before copying it
Understanding Cohesion RL. K 5-10	Sentence Completion - Fill in the Blank Students will be able to use word recall and word choice.	Teacher says the sentence out loud and students raise their hand to guess the missing word.
Understanding Cohesion RL. K 5-10	Sentence Completion - Fill in the Blank Students will be able to use word recall and word choice.	Teacher says the sentence out loud and students raise their hand to guess the missing word.
Supporting Opinions S.L. K. 4-10	Assessment/Error Detection - True or False Students practice yes or no and critical thinking skills	Dictation or chose any of the assignments for a quiz
Write, draw and compose short informational texts SL.K. 4-10	Composition - Write a new sentence Students will be able to develop writing skills to use complete thoughts	Students can use media or a picture to prompt their sentence compositions
Interrogative Sentences WHST 7.1	Translation - Translate questions Students will practice new vocabulary for interrogative sentences	Students can use media or a dictionary or work in groups to translate together
Retell texts and recount experiences using select key words W.K. 5-10 SL.K.4-10	Recollection – Rewrite the Questions Students will be able to rewrite questions.	Teacher can model first part of the sentence and leave it to students to guess the conclusion. Students can work in groups or with a partner to create new sentences.

Directions in English: Write in Your Language
Directions in Chinese:用中文写
Directions in Spanish: Escribe En Tu Idioma
Directions in Korea: 한글

Hello! Hi!

Good morning!

Good afternoon!

Good evening!

Welcome!

In order to learn a language fast, you must make sure that you know all of the Alphabet letters perfectly.

为了快速学习语言，你必须确保你完全了解所有的英文字母。

Para aprender un idioma rápido, debes asegurarte de que conoces perfectamente todas las letras del alfabeto.

영어를 빨리 배우려면 모든 알파벳 글자를 완벽하게 알아야합니다.

Chapter 1
Alphabet
Chinese: 字母
Spanish: Alfabeto
Korean: 알파벳

A	B	C	D	E
F	G	H	I	J
K	L	M	N	O
P	Q	R	S	T
U	V	W	X	Y
Z				

A		C		E
	G		I	
K		M		O
	Q		S	
U		W		Y

	B		D	
F		H		J
	L		N	
P		R		T
	V		X	
Z				

Directions in English: Write the Missing Capital Letters
Directions in Chinese: 填写正确的大写字母
Directions in Spanish: Completar Las Letras Que Desaparecido
Directions in Korean: 빈칸에 알맞은 영어 대문자를 채워 넣으시오.

A				
Z				

a	b	c	d	e
f	g	h	i	j
k	l	m	n	o
p	q	r	s	t
u	v	w	x	y
z				

Directions in English: **Fill in the missing lowercase letters.**
Directions in Chinese: 小写字母
Directions in Spanish: **Completa las Letras Minúsculas**
Directions in Korean: 빈칸에 알맞은 영어 소문자를 채워 넣으시오.

	b		d	
f		h		j
	l		n	
p		r		t
	v		x	
z				

Directions in English: Fill in the missing lowercase letters.
Directions in Chinese: 小写字母
Directions in Spanish: Completa las Letras Minúsculas
Directions in Korean: 빈칸에 알맞은 영어 소문자를 채워 넣으시오.

a		c		e
	g		i	
k		m		o
	q		s	
u		w		y

Directions in English: Fill in the missing lowercase letters.
Directions in Chinese: 小写字母
Directions in Spanish: Completa las Letras Minúsculas
Directions in Korean: 빈칸에 알맞은 영어 소문자를 채워 넣으시오.

a				
z				

In order to learn a language, you must understand the sounds of the language. In English, we call this Phonics.

为了学习一种语言，你必须理解语言的声音。我们称之为Phonics。

Para aprender un idioma rápido, debe comprender la fonética del idioma.

언어를 배우려면 언어의 소리를 이해해야합니다. 영어로 우리는 이것을 Phonics 라고 부릅니다.

Chapter 2
Phonics
Chinese:语音和字母表
Spanish: Fónica
Korean:파닉스

Directions in English: Read Aloud the Phonics Sounda (You may go to Youtube for assistance)
Directions in Chinese: 大声朗读。
Directions in Spanish: Leer en Ingles
Directions in Korean: 알파벳 (크게 읽으시오)

B	D	F	G	H
J	K	L	M	N
P	Q	R	S	T
V	W	Y	Z	

2a. Consonants And Vowels

B				**H**
	K			
P			**S**	

Y

Directions in English: Read Aloud the Blends (You may go to Youtube for assistance)
Directions in Chinese: 大声朗读。
Directions in Spanish: Leer en Ingles
Directions in Korean: 알파벳 (크게 읽으시오)

bl	**br**	
cl	**cr**	**ch**
dr	**dw**	
fl	**fr**	
gl	**gr**	**gh**
pl	**pr**	**ph**
sh	**sl**	**str**
tr	**tw**	**th**
wh	**wr**	**wy**

Consonant Blends

Directions in English: Write the Blends for the Following Consonants
Directions in Chinese: 写两个辅音。
Directions in Spanish: Escribir las mezclas para las siguientes consonantes
Directions in Korean: 이 소리들을연습하시오.

bl	br			**B**				
cl	ch	cr		**C**				
dr	dw			**D**				
fl	fr			**G**				
gl	gr	gh		**P**				
pl	pr	ph		**Q**				
st	str			**S**				
sh	sl	shr	sw	**S**				
th	tr	tw		**T**				
wh	wr			**W**				

A	E	I	O	U

2e. Vowels

ah	bat	cat	data	chat
fat	hat	jack	lack	mat
pat	quack	rat	sat	that

Directions in Chinese: 在同一列中写下具有类似拼写字母的单词。
Directions in Spanish: Escriba las palabras que tienen letras deletreadas similares en la misma columna.
Directions in Korean: 알파벳 /U/는 장모음 U와 소리가 같습니다.

at	bat	cat	back	chat
fat	hat	jack	lack	mat
pat	quack	rat	sat	that

at	back

2g. Short A Sounds

ate	bay	cake	day	fake
gate	hate	late	mate	rate
state	wait	late	plate	Jake

2g. Long A vowels sound like their Alphabet letter /A/

Directions in Chinese: 在同一列中写下具有类似拼写字母的单词。
Directions in Spanish: Escriba las palabras que tienen letras deletreadas similares en la misma columna.
Directions in Korean: 알파벳 /U/는 장모음 U와 소리가 같습니다.

ate	bay	crate	day	fate
gate	hate	late	mate	rate
state	clay	play	plate	slay

ate	bay

aw	**claw**	**draw**	**gawk**	**because**
maw	**paw**	**raw**	**saw**	**pause**
bawl	**jaw**	**hawk**	**law**	**clause**

29

2h. AW or AU usually sound the same

Directions in Chinese: 在同一列中写下具有类似拼写字母的单词。
Directions in Spanish: Escriba las palabras que tienen letras deletreadas similares en la misma columna.
Directions in Korean: 알파벳 /U/는 장모음 U와 소리가 같습니다.

aw	claw	draw	gawk	because
bawk	paw	raw	saw	pause
bawl	jaw	hawk	law	clause

aw	pause	gawk

egg	beg	check	dead	head
fed	get	shed	led	read
instead	wed	bed	ahead	leg

2i. Short E words sound like /Eh/

egg	beg	check	instead	head
fed	get	shed	led	read
dead	wreck	bed	ahead	leg

egg	head	check

2i. Short E Sounds

each	beach	deed	feed	heed
lead	meet	need	please	read
seed	tea	peach	week	reach

each	beach	deed	feed	heed
lead	meet	need	please	read
seed	tea	peach	week	reach

each	deed	lead

it	bit	chick	flick	fish
Is	his	git	hit	lit
mitt	nick	pick	Rick	sick
stick	ticket	Vic	wish	zip

2k. Short I vowels sound like /is/

35

it	bit	chick	flick	fish
Is	his	git	hit	lit
miss	nick	pick	Rick	sick
stick	ticket	Vic	wish	zip

it	chick	is

bike	alright	dice	fight	hike
like	Mike	might	night	light
pie	quiet	right	sight	tight

21. Long I Vowels sound like their Alphabet letter /I/

bike	alright	dice	fight	hike
like	Mike	might	night	light
slice	quiet	right	sight	tight

bike	alright	dice

bought	cot	daughter	fought	hot
lot	naught	pot	sought	not
taught	dock	brought	got	dots
robots	body	clod	clock	jock

Directions in Chinese: 在同一列中写下具有类似拼写字母的单词。
Directions in Spanish: Escriba las palabras que tienen letras deletreadas similares en la misma columna.
Directions in Korean: 알파벳 /U/는 장모음 U와 소리가 같습니다.

bought	cot	daughter	fought	hot
lot	lock	pot	rot	sought
taught	dock	brought	got	dots
robots	body	clod	clock	jock

bought	cot	clock

boat	coat	dole	float	goat
hotel	joke	motel	note	poke
quote	rote	soak	Coke	wrote

2k. Long O words make the same sound as the Alphabet letter O/ O /

Directions in English: Write the words that have similar spelling into the same column.
Directions in Chinese: 在同一列中写下具有类似拼写字母的单词。
Directions in Spanish: Escriba las palabras que tienen letras deletreadas similares en la misma columna.
Directions in Korean: 알파벳 /U/는 장모음 U와 소리가 같습니다.

boat	coat	dole	float	goat
hotel	joke	motel	note	poke
quote	rote	soak	Coke	wrote

boat	joke	quote

Directions in English: Read Aloud the Phonics Sounda (You may go to Youtube for assistance)
Directions in Chinese: 大声朗读。
Directions in Spanish: Leer en Ingles
Directions in Korean: 알파벳 (크게 읽으시오)

boot	cool	booth	bloom	food
fool	loot	tooth	pool	roof
too	hoot	do	goo	moo

| boot | cool | booth | bloom | food |
| loot | tooth | pool | roof |
| fool |
| too | hoot | do | goo | moo |

boot	cool	booth

Directions in English: Read Aloud the Phonics Sounda (You may go to Youtube for assistance)
Directions in Chinese: 大声朗读。
Directions in Spanish: Leer en Ingles
Directions in Korean: 알파벳 (크게 읽으시오)

up	cup	dull	full	lull
mull	null	pull	pup	strut
tut	cub	rub	hub	pub

Directions in Chinese: 在同一列中写下具有类似拼写字母的单词。
Directions in Spanish: Escriba las palabras que tienen letras deletreadas similares en la misma columna.
Directions in Korean: 알파벳 /U/는 장모음 U와 소리가 같습니다.

up	cup	dull	full	lull
mull	null	pull	pup	strut
tut	cub	rub	hub	pub

up	dull	cub

Directions in English: Read Aloud the Phonics Sounda (You may go to Youtube for assistance)
Directions in Chinese: 大声朗读。
Directions in Spanish: Leer en Ingles
Directions in Korean: 알파벳 (크게 읽으시오)

astute	blue	cute	fluke	hue
Lou	mule	puke	glue	music
you	duke	flute	due	clue

Directions in English: Write the words with similar spelling into the same column.
Directions in Chinese: 在同一列中写下具有类似拼写字母的单词。
Directions in Spanish: Escriba las palabras que tienen letras deletreadas similares en la misma columna.
Directions in Korean: 알파벳 /U/는 장모음 U와 소리가 같습니다.

astute	blue	cute	fluke	hue
Lou	mule	puke	glue	music
you	duke	flute	due	clue

blue	duke	you

Directions in English: Read Aloud the Phonics Sounda (You may go to Youtube for assistance)
Directions in Chinese: 大声朗读。
Directions in Spanish: Leer en Ingles
Directions in Korean: 알파벳 (크게 읽으시오

blush	crush	fuss	flush	gush
hush	lush	push	put	but
mug	gut	plush	fudge	hug

blush	crush	fuss	flush	bug
hush	lush	push	put	but
mug	gut	plush	fudge	hug

blush	put	mug

2p. Other U Sounds

In order to learn a language fast, you must make sure that you know all of the Numbers very well.

你必须学习如何用英语写数字。

Para aprender un idioma rápido, debes asegurarte de que conoces todos los Números muy bien.

언어를 빨리 배우려면 모든 수를 잘 알아야합니다.

Chapter 3
How to Write Numbers
如何写数字
Cómo Escribir Números
숫자 와 서수

English	English	Numbers 1-10 Directions in English: Write in Your Language Directions in Chinese: 中文写。 Directions in Spanish: Escribe En Tu Idioma Directions in Korea: 한글
1	one	uno
1	one	
2	two	
3	three	
4	four	
5	five	
6	six	
7	seven	
8	eight	
9	nine	
10	ten	

English	English	Numbers 1-10 Directions in English: Write 3 times in English Directions in Chinese: 写3次 Directions in Spanish: Escribe en Ingles Directions in Korean: 영어로 3 번 쓰기
1	one	One one one
1	one	
2	two	
3	three	
4	four	
5	five	
6	six	
7	seven	
8	eight	
9	nine	
10	ten	

Directions in English: Read Aloud the Phonics Sounda (You may go to Youtube for assistance)
Directions in Chinese: 大声朗读。
Directions in Spanish: Leer en Ingles
Directions in Korean:알파벳 (크게 읽으시오

1	2	3	4	5
6	7	8	9	10
11	12	13	14	15
16	17	18	19	20

English	English	Numbers 11-20 **Directions in English: Write in Your Language** **Directions in Chinese:**用中文写。 **Directions in Spanish: Escribe En Tu Idioma** **Directions in Korea:** 한글
11	**eleven**	
12	**twelve**	
13	**thirteen**	
14	**fourteen**	
15	**fifteen**	
16	**sixteen**	
17	**seventeen**	
18	**eighteen**	
19	**nineteen**	
20	**twenty**	

English	English	Numbers 11-20 Directions in English: Write 3 times Directions in Chinese: 写3次 Directions in Spanish: Escribe en Ingles Directions in Korean: 영어로 3 번 쓰기
11	eleven	**Eleven eleven eleven**
11	eleven	
12	twelve	
13	thirteen	
14	fourteen	
15	fifteen	
16	sixteen	
17	seventeen	
18	eighteen	
19	nineteen	
20	twenty	

	2		4	
6		8		10
	12		14	
16		18		20

1		3		5
	7		9	
11		13		15
	17		19	
21				

3c. Numbers

1				
				20

Directions in English: Read Aloud (You may go to Youtube for assistance)
Directions in Chinese: 大声朗读。
Directions in Spanish: Leer en Ingles
Directions in Korean:알파벳 (크게 읽으시오

10	20	30	40	50
60	70	80	90	100

3e. Numbers By Tens

10				
				100

English	English	Numbers by Tens Directions in English: Write in Your Language Directions in Chinese:用中文写。 Directions in Spanish: Escribe En Tu Idioma Directions in Korea: 한글
10	ten	diez
10	ten	
20	twenty	
30	thirty	
40	forty	
50	fifty	
60	sixty	
70	seventy	
80	eighty	
90	ninety	
100	One hundred	

English	English	Numbers by Tens Directions in English: Write 3 times Directions in Chinese: 写3次 Directions in Spanish: Escribe en Ingles Directions in Korean: 영어로 3 번 쓰기
10	**ten**	**Ten ten ten**
10	**ten**	
20	**twenty**	
30	**thirty**	
40	**forty**	
50	**fifty**	
60	**sixty**	
70	**seventy**	
80	**eighty**	
90	**ninety**	
100	**One hundred**	

In order to learn a language fast, you must learn the ordinals and orders of numbers.
为了快速学习一门语言，你必须学习序数和数字顺序。
Para aprender un idioma rápido, debes aprender los ordinales y las órdenes de los números.
언어를 빨리 배우려면 숫자의 서수와 순서를 알아야합니다.

Chapter 4
How to Write Ordinals
如何编写序号
Cómo Escribir Ordinales
서수

Ordinals show order of events or place.	Ordinals in Sentences Directions in English: Write in Your Language Directions in Chinese:用中文写。 Directions in Spanish: Escribe En Tu Idioma Directions in Korea: 한글
Mary was first.	
Mary was first.	
John was second.	
Peter was third.	
	Ordinals in Sentences Directions in English: Write 3 times Directions in Chinese: 写3次 Directions in Spanish: Escribe en Ingles Directions in Korean: 영어로 3 번 쓰기
Mary was first.	
John was second.	
Peter was third.	

English	English	Ordinals Directions in English: Write in Your Language Directions in Chinese:用中文写。 Directions in Spanish: Escribe En Tu Idioma Directions in Korea: 한글
1	first	primero
1	first	
2	second	
3	third	
4	fourth	
5	fifth	
6	sixth	
7	seventh	
8	eighth	
9	ninth	
10	tenth	

English	English	Ordinals **Directions in English:** Write 3 times **Directions in Chinese:** 写3次 **Directions in Spanish:** Escribe en Ingles **Directions in Korean:** 영어로 3 번 쓰기
1	first	**First first first**
1	first	
2	second	
3	third	
4	fourth	
5	fifth	
6	sixth	
7	seventh	
8	eighth	
9	ninth	
10	tenth	

English	Days of the Week Directions in English: Write in Your Language Directions in Chinese:用中文写。 Directions in Spanish: Escribe En Tu Idioma Directions in Korea: 한글
Monday	Lunes
Monday	
Tuesday	
Wednesday	
Thursday	
Friday	

English	Days of the Week Directions in English: Write 3 times Directions in Chinese: 写3次 Directions in Spanish: Escribe en Ingles Directions in Korean: 영어로 3 번 쓰기
Monday	**Monday Monday Monday**
Monday	
Tuesday	
Wednesday	
Thursday	
Friday	

English	Ordinal	Using Ordinals with Days of the Week Directions in English: Write in Your Language Directions in Chinese:用中文写。 Directions in Spanish: Escribe En Tu Idioma Directions in Korea: 한글
Monday	first	Monday is the first day of the school week. El lunes es el primer día de la semana escolar.
Monday	first	
Tuesday	second	
Wednesday	third	
Thursday	fourth	
Friday	fifth	

English	English	Using Ordinals with Days of the Week Directions in English: Write 1 time Directions in Chinese: 写次 Directions in Spanish: Escribe en Ingles Directions in Korean: 영어로 번 쓰기
Monday	first	Monday is the first day of the school week.
Monday	first	
Tuesday	second	
Wednesday	third	
Thursday	fourth	
Friday	fifth	

English	The Days Of The 5 Day School Week Directions in English: Write 3 times Directions in Chinese: 写3次 Directions in Spanish: Escribe en Ingles Directions in Korean: 영어로 3 번 쓰기
First	**Monday**
First	
Second	
Third	
Fourth	
Fifth	

English	Days of the 7 day week Directions in English: Read Aloud (You may go to Youtube for assistance) Directions in Chinese: 大声朗读。 Directions in Spanish: Leer en Ingles Directions in Korean: 알파벳 (크게 읽으시오)
First	**Sunday**
Second	**Monday**
Third	**Tuesday**
Fourth	**Wednesday**
Fifth	**Thursday**
Sixth	**Friday**
Seventh	**Saturday**

English	Write The Days Of The 7 Day Week Directions in English: Write in Your Language Directions in Chinese:用中文写。 Directions in Spanish: Escribe En Tu Idioma Directions in Korea: 한글
Sunday	
Sunday	
Monday	
Tuesday	
Wednesday	
Thursday	
Friday	
Saturday	

English	Write The Days Of The 7 Day Week Directions in English: Write 3 times Directions in Chinese: 写3次 Directions in Spanish: Escribe en Ingles Directions in Korean: 영어로 3 번 쓰기
Sunday	
Monday	
Tuesday	
Wednesday	
Thursday	
Friday	
Saturday	

English	Months	Months of the Year Directions in English: Write in Your Language Directions in Chinese:用中文写。 Directions in Spanish: Escribe En Tu Idioma Directions in Korea: 한글
first	January	
second	February	
third	March	
fourth	April	
fifth	May	
sixth	June	
seventh	July	
eighth	August	
ninth	September	
tenth	October	
eleventh	November	
twelfth	December	

Months

Months of the Year
Directions in English: Write 3 times
Directions in Chinese: 写3次
Directions in Spanish: Escribe en Ingles
Directions in Korean: 영어로 3 번 쓰기

January	January January January
January	
February	
March	
April	
May	
June	
July	
August	
September	
October	
November	
December	

English	English	Ordinals By Tenths Directions in English: Write in Your Language Directions in Chinese:用中文写。 Directions in Spanish: Escribe En Tu Idioma Directions in Korea: 한글
10	tenth	
20	twentieth	
30	thirtieth	
40	fortieth	
50	fiftieth	
60	sixtieth	
70	seventieth	
80	eightieth	
90	ninetieth	
100	One hundredth	

English	English	Ordinals by Tenths Directions in English: Write 3 times Directions in Chinese: 写3次 Directions in Spanish: Escribe en Ingles Directions in Korean: 영어로 3 번 쓰기
20	twentieth	twentieth twentieth twentieth
20	twentieth	
30	thirtieth	
40	fortieth	
50	fiftieth	
60	sixtieth	
70	seventieth	
80	eightieth	
90	ninetieth	
100	One hundredth	

In order to learn a language fast, you must pronouns and conjugations and subjects and the correct verb usage.

为了快速学习语言，你必须使用代词，动词和主语以及正确的动词用法。

Para aprender un idioma rápido, debes pronombres y los sujetos y los sujetos corrigen el uso del verbo.

언어를 빨리 배우려면 올바른 동사와 함께 대명사를 사용해야합니다.

Chapter 5
How to Call People
如何解决使用代词的人
Cómo dirigirse a personas usando pronombres
사람을 호칭하는 방법

English	Pronouns Directions in English: Write in Your Language Directions in Chinese:用中文写。 Directions in Spanish: Escribe En Tu Idioma Directions in Korea: 한글
I	
I	
You	
He	
She	
It	
We	
They	

English	Pronouns Directions in English: Write 3 times Directions in Chinese: 写3次 Directions in Spanish: Escribe en Ingles Directions in Korean: 영어로 **3** 번 쓰기
I	I I I
I	
You	
He	
She	
It	
We	
They	

Directions in English: Write 3 times
Directions in Chinese: 写3次
Directions in Spanish: Escribe en Ingles
Directions in Korean: 영어로 3 번 쓰기

Pronouns in Sentences
Directions in English: Write in Your Language
Directions in Chinese:用中文写。
Directions in Spanish: Escribe En Tu Idioma
Directions in Korea: 한글

1. I am Sam.

Me llamo Sam.

_____

_____

_____

_____

_____

_____

I am a student.

Soy un estudiante.

1._____

2._____

3._____

1._____

2._____

3._____

Directions in English: Write 3 times
Directions in Chinese: 写3次
Directions in Spanish: Escribe en Ingles
Directions in Korean: 영어로 3 번 쓰기

Directions in English: Write in Your Language
Directions in Chinese: 用中文写。
Directions in Spanish: Escribe En Tu Idioma
Directions in Korea: 한글

You are the teacher.

1._____
2._____
3._____

Eres un maestro.

1._____
2._____
3._____

Directions in English: Write 3 times
Directions in Chinese: 写3次
Directions in Spanish: Escribe en Ingles
Directions in Korean: 영어로 3 번 쓰기

Directions in English: Write in Your Language
Directions in Chinese: 用中文写
Directions in Spanish: Escribe En Tu Idioma
Directions in Korea: 한글

He is my brother.

1._____
2._____
3._____

Él es mi hermano.

1._____
2._____
3._____

Directions in English: Write 3 times
Directions in Chinese: 写3次
Directions in Spanish: Escribe en Ingles
Directions in Korean: 영어로 3 번 쓰기

Directions in English: Write in Your Language
Directions in Chinese: 用中文写
Directions in Spanish: Escribe En Tu Idioma
Directions in Korea: 한글

She is my sister.

1._____
2._____
3._____

Ella es mi hermana.

1._____
2._____
3._____

Directions in English: Write 3 times
Directions in Chinese: 写3次
Directions in Spanish: Escribe en Ingles
Directions in Korean: 영어로 3 번 쓰기

Directions in English: Write in Your Language
Directions in Chinese: 用中文写
Directions in Spanish: Escribe En Tu Idioma
Directions in Korea: 한글

It is good.

1._____

2._____

3._____

Es bueno.

1._____

2._____

3._____

Directions in English: Write 3 times
Directions in Chinese: 写3次
Directions in Spanish: Escribe en Ingles
Directions in Korean: 영어로 **3** 번 쓰기

Directions in English: Write in Your Language
Directions in Chinese: 用中文写
Directions in Spanish: Escribe En Tu Idioma
Directions in Korea: 한글

We are happy.

1._____

2._____

3._____

Estamos felices.

1._____

2._____

3._____

Directions in English: Write 3 times
Directions in Chinese: 写3次
Directions in Spanish: Escribe en Ingles
Directions in Korean: 영어로 3 번 쓰기

Directions in English: Write in Your Language
Directions in Chinese: 用中文写
Directions in Spanish: Escribe En Tu Idioma
Directions in Korea: 한글

They are nice.

1._____
2._____
3._____

Ellos son agradables.

1._____
2._____
3._____

Quiz

Directions in English: **What are the 7 pronouns?**
Directions in Chinese: **7**个代词是什么？
Directions in Spanish: **7¿Cuáles son los 7 pronombres?**
Directions in Korean: 7가지 대명사는 무엇입니까?

1._____

2._____

3._____

4._____

5._____

6._____

7._____

Directions in English: **Write the missing word in English**
Directions in Chinese: 填空
Directions in Spanish:**¿Cuál es la palabra faltante?**
Directions in Korean: 다음 빈칸에 알맞을 말을 채워 넣으시오.

1._____ **am Sam.**
2._____ **am a student.**
3._____ **are the teacher.**
4._____ **is my brother.**
5._____ **is my sister.**
6._____ **is good.**
7._____ **are happy.**
8._____**are nice.**

English	Directions in English: Write in Your Language Directions in Chinese:用中文写 Directions in Spanish: Escribe En Tu Idioma Directions in Korea: 한글
	1. Yo soy
1. I am **2. You are** **3. He is** **4. She is** **5. It is** **6. We are** **7. They are**	**1.**_____ **2.**_____ **3.**_____ **4.**_____ **5.**_____ **6.**_____ **7.**_____

English	Directions in English: Write 1 time
	Directions in Chinese: 写次
	Directions in Spanish: Escribe en Ingles
	Directions in Korean: 영어로 번 쓰기

1. I am

1. I am
2. You are
3. He is
4. She is
5. It is
6. We are
7. They are

1. _____
2. _____
3. _____
4. _____
5. _____
6. _____
7. _____

5q. Every Pronoun Has A Right Verb Called A Conjugation

Directions in English: Write in the verb from Page 88
Directions in Chinese: 写入第88页的动词
Directions in Spanish: Escriba el verbo de la página 88
Directions in Korean: 동사에 88 쪽부터 씁니다.

1. I _____ Sam.
2. I _____ a student.
3. You _____ a teacher.
4. He _____ my brother.
5. She _____ my sister.
6. It _____ good.
7. We _____ happy.
8. They _____ nice.

5r. Conjugations

Directions in English: Fill in the sentence.
Directions in Chinese: 填上句子。
Directions in Spanish: Completa la oración.
Directions in Korean: 다음 빈칸에 알맞을 말을 채워 넣으시오

1. I am _____.
2. I am a _____.
3. You are a _____.
4. He is my _____.
5. She is my _____.
6. It is _____.
7. We are _____.
8. They are _____.

Directions in English: Put the words in order
Directions in Chinese: 什么是正确的句子？
Directions in Spanish: ¿Cuál es la oración correcta?
Directions in Korean: 알맞은 순서대로 빈칸을 채우시오.

1. Sam am I

_____ .

2. am student I a

_____ .

3. you a teacher are

_____ .

4. my he brother is

_____ .

5. is it good

_____ .

6. Happy we are

_____ .

In order to learn a language fast, you must memorize the parts of the body.
为了快速学习语言，你必须记住身体的各个部分。
Para aprender un idioma rápido, debes memorizar las partes del cuerpo.
언어를 빨리 배우려면 신체의 각 부분을 외워야합니다.

Chapter 6
How to Talk about your Body
如何谈论你的身体
Cómo Hablar Sobre Tu Cuerpo
신체를 명명하는 방법

English	Directions in English: Write in Your Language Directions in Chinese:用中文写 Directions in Spanish: Escribe En Tu Idioma Directions in Korea: 한글
1. Head/Hair	Cabeza/Cabello
1. Head/Hair	
2. Neck	
3. Chest/Back	
4. Arm/Hand/Finger	
5. Leg/Knee/Foot / Toe	
6. Knee	

English	Directions in English: Write 3 times Directions in Chinese: 写3次 Directions in Spanish: Escribe en Ingles Directions in Korean: 영어로 3 번 쓰기
Head/hair	**Head/hair**
1. Head/Hair	
2. Neck	
3. Chest/Back	
4. Arm/Elbow/Hand/Finger	
5. Leg/Knee/Foot/Toe	
6. Butt	

Your Body

Directions in English: What are the main body parts in English?
Directions in Chinese:身体的主要部分是什么？
Directions in Spanish: ¿Cuáles son las partes del cuerpo en inglés?
Directions in Korean: 영어로 된 신체 부분은 무엇입니까?

1. Hair/Head

1._____/_____

2._____

3._____/_____

4._____/_____/_____
_____

5._____/_____/_____
_____

6._____

English	Directions in English: Write in Your Language Directions in Chinese:用中文写 Directions in Spanish: Escribe En Tu Idioma Directions in Korea: 한글
Brain	
Brain	
Eyes	
Eyebrows	
Nose	
Mouth/Lips	
Teeth	
Ears	
Cheeks	

English	Directions in English: Write 3 times Directions in Chinese: 写3次 Directions in Spanish: Escribe en Ingles Directions in Korean: 영어로 3 번 쓰기
Brain	**Brain Brain Brain**
Brain	
Eyes	
Eyebrows	
Nose	
Mouth	
Lips	
Teeth	
Ears	
Cheeks	

Your Head Parts

Directions in English: What are the main head parts in English?
Directions in Chinese: 英语中头部的部分是什么？
Directions in Spanish: ¿Cuáles son las partes de la cabeza en inglés?
Directions in Korean: 머리 부분은 영어로 무엇입니까?

1._____
2._____
3._____
4._____
5._____
6._____
7._____
8._____
9._____

In order to learn a language fast, you must understand how to use the sentence structures.

为了快速学习语言，您必须了解如何使用句子结构。

Cada oración tiene un sujeto, un verbo y un pensamiento completo.

언어를 빨리 배우기 위해서, 당신은 문장구조를 사용하는 방법을 반드시 배워야 합니다.

Chapter 7
How To Make Sentences
如何制作句子
Cómo Hacer Oraciones
문장을 구성하는 방법

- **All sentences have a subject, a verb and a complement/complete thought.**
- 所有的句子都有一个主语和一个谓语。
- **Todas las oraciones tienen un sujeto y un predicado.**
- 모든 문장에는 주어, 동사, 그리고 보어가 있습니다.

Subject Sujeta 名词主语 주어	Verb Verbo 动词 동사	Complete Thought Pensamientos Completos 述语 보어
I	am	happy.

Directions in English: Write in Your Language
Directions in Chinese: 用中文写
Directions in Spanish: Escribe En Tu Idioma
Directions in Korea: 한글

Yo	estoy	feliz.

7a. Sentence Parts

Subject	Verb	Complement
I	am	happy.
You	are	ten.
He	is	thirty.

Directions in English: Write 1 time
Directions in Chinese: 写1次
Directions in Spanish: Escribe en Ingles
Directions in Korean: 영어로 1번 쓰기

Subject	Verb	Complement
I	am	happy.
You	are	ten.
He	is	thirty.

I	you	The girl
我	你	那位女孩

The man	A state	The book

He	Americans	California

Directions in English: Write 1 time
Directions in Chinese: 写1次
Directions in Spanish: Escribe en Ingles
Directions in Korean: 영어로 1번 쓰기

I	you	The girl
The man	A state	The book
He	Americans	California

The teacher	The student	The professor
老师	学生	教授
The teacher	The student	The professor
The principal	Your classroom	The board
A pencil	The school	The bathroom

Directions in English: Write 1 time
Directions in Chinese: 写1次
Directions in Spanish: Escribe en Ingles
Directions in Korean: 영어로 1번 쓰기

The teacher	The student	The professor
老师	学生	教授
The teacher	The student	The professor
The principal	Your classroom	The board
A pencil	The school	The bathroom

My home	My family	My house
我的家	我的家人	我的房子
My home	My family	My house
My room	My keys	My purse
My friend	My stuff	My desk

Directions in English: Write 1 time
Directions in Chinese: 写1次
Directions in Spanish: Escribe en Ingles
Directions in Korean: 영어로 1번 쓰기

My home	My family	My house
My room	My keys	My purse
My friend	My stuff	My desk

Directions in English: Write in Your Language
Directions in Chinese:用中文写
Directions in Spanish: Escribe En Tu Idioma
Directions in Korea: 한글

am	are	is
是	是	是
am	are	is
say	start	learn
study	go	write

Directions in English: Write 1 time
Directions in Chinese: 写1次
Directions in Spanish: Escribe en Ingles
Directions in Korean: 영어로 1번 쓰기

am	**are**	**is**
say	**start**	**learn**
study	**go**	**write**

am	**I am <u>at school</u>.** complement
are	**We are <u>new students</u>.** complement
say	**We say <u>the words</u>.** complement
go	**I go <u>to the park</u>.** complement
study	**I study <u>a lot</u>.** complement

I am <u>at school</u>.
complement

1. I am at school.

2. We are new students.

3. We say the words.

4. I go to the park.

5. I study a lot.

Directions in English: Write the Complements from the previous page.
Directions in Chinese: 填写
Directions in Spanish: Escribe las complementos.
Directions in Korean: 앞장에서 사용한 보어를 빈칸에 채우시오.

1. I am _____.

2. We are _____.

3. We say _____.

4. I go _____.

5 I study _____.

In order to learn a language fast, you must learn learn how to ask simple questions! 为了学习一门语言，你必须学习如何提出问题。Para aprender un idioma debes aprender a hacer preguntas. 언어를 빨리 배우려면 간단한 질문을하는 법을 배워야합니다!

Directions in English: How To Make Questions - Read Aloud
Directions in Chinese: 如何提出问题 - 阅读或说话。
Directions in Spanish: Cómo hacer preguntas — Leer
Directions in Korean: 질문을하는 법 - 소리내어 읽는 법

Question starters	verbs	Nouns subjects	Question endings
Who	are	you	?
What	is	your name	?
When	is	the class	?
Where	are	my keys	?
Why	did	she leave	?
How	can	I do this	?

Directions in English: Write these questions in your language.
Directions in Chinese: 用中文写下这些问题。
Directions in Spanish: Escribe estas preguntas en tu idioma.
Directions in Korea:

Question starters	verbs	Nouns subjects	Question endings
Who	are	you	?
What	is	your name	?
When	is	the class	?
Where	are	my keys	?
Why	did	she leave	?
How	can	I do this	?

Directions in English: Write the question starters in your English.
Directions in Chinese: 用英语写下问题的开头。
Directions in Spanish: Escriba los iniciadores de preguntas en su inglés.
Directions in Korean: 질문 부분을 영어로 작성하십시오.

Question starters	verbs	Nouns subjects	Question endings
	are	you	?
	is	your name	?
	is	the class	?
	are	my keys	?
	did	she leave	?
	can	I do this	?

In order to learn a language fast, you must learn many verbs for the major actions in your life!

为了快速学习英语，你必须为你的生活行为学习许多动词。

¡Para aprender un idioma rápido, debes aprender muchos verbos para las acciones en tu vida!

언어를 빨리 배우려면 인생의 주요 행동에 대한 여러 동사를 배워야합니다!

Chapter 8
How To Talk About Your Life
如何谈论你的生活
Cómo Hablar Sobre Las Acciones De Tu Vida
당신의 매일의 삶의 동작을 표현 하는 방법

Body Verbs

Directions in English: Write in Your Language
Directions in Chinese:用中文写
Directions in Spanish: Escribe En Tu Idioma
Directions in Korea: 한글

1. Lie down	
2. Get up	
3. Go	
4. Come	
5. Arrive	
6. Live	
7. Wake up	
8. Go to bed	
9. Stay	
10. Succeed	

Body Verbs

Directions in English: Write 3 times
Directions in Chinese: 写3次
Directions in Spanish: Escribe en Ingles
Directions in Korean: 영어로 3 번 쓰기

Lie down	
Get up	
Go	
Come	
Arrive	
Live	
Wake up	
Go to bed	
Stay	
Succeed	

8b. Whole Body Verbs

Body Verbs

GUESS THE VOCABULARY WORD
Directions in English: Guess the vocabulary word.
Directions in Chinese: 猜猜这个单词。
Directions in Spanish: Intenta descifrar la palabra del vocabulario.
Directions in Korean: 단어를 알아내시오.

ile wndo	
etg pu	
og	
eomc	
rvirae	
evil	
pu kwae	
og ot dbe	
yats	
cedcsue	

8c. Whole Body Verbs

BRAIN VERBS	I	YOU	HE/SHE/IT (add s)	WE	THEY
Lie down	I lie down	You lie down	He or she lies down	We lie down	They lie down
Lie down					
Get up					
Go					
Come					
Arrive					
Take					
Wake up					
Go to bed					
Stay					
Succeed					

8d. Whole Body Verbs – Conjugations - Find the right verb写下合适的动词。
Encuentra el verbo apropiado para el pronombre대명사에 적절한 동사를 찾으십시오.

127

Body Verbs

Lie down	I lie down at night.
Get up	I get up at 6 am.
Go	I go to the bank.
Come	I come home late.
Arrive	The teacher arrives early.
Take	I take the bus.
Wake up	I wake up on time.
Go to bed	I go to bed at 9 pm.
Stay	I stay with a family.
Succeed	I always succeed.

Body Verbs

Directions in English: Copy The Sentence from the previous page
Directions in Chinese: 写下句子。
Directions in Spanish: Escribe la oracEón de la página anterior.
Directions in Korean: 이전 페이지에서 배운 문장을 다시 작성하시오.

Lie down

Get up

Go

Come

Arrive

Take

Wake up

Go to bed

Stay

Succeed

8f. Whole Body Verbs

Body Verbs

Directions in English: Fill In The Sentence
Directions in Chinese: 用模型句子中的正确单词填充句子。
Directions in Spanish: Completa la oración con las palabras correctas de las oraciones modelo.
Directions in Korean: 문장을 완성하시오.

Lie down	I ____ ____ at night.
Get up	I ____ ____ at 6 am.
Go	I __ to the bank.
Come	I ____ home late.
Arrive	The teacher _____ early.
Take	I ____ the bus.
Wake up	I ____ ___ on time.
Go to bed	I __ __ ___ at 9 pm.
Stay	I ____ with a family.
Succeed	I _____ succeed.

8g. Whole Body Verbs

Body Verbs

Lie down	**I lie down___ _____.**
Get up	**I get up ____ ____.**
Go	**I go ____ ____ _____.**
Come	**I come _____ _____.**
Arrive	**The teacher _____ early.**
Take	**I take _____ _____.**
Wake up	**I wake up ____ ____.**
Go to bed	**I go to bed ___ ____.**
Stay	**I stay ___ ____ _____.**
Succeed	**I always _____.**

Body verbs

Directions in English: True / False ∘ Put T or F Below
Directions in Chinese: 在下面写正确或不正确 写T为正确或F为不正确。
Directions in Spanish: Escribe T si es verdadero, F si es falso
Directions in Korean: 참이면 T / 거짓이면 F 를 적으시오

1. Lie Down	I lie down on paper.
2. Get up	I get up at 12:00 noon.
3. Go	He goes to the cup.
4. Come	I come to the sink at 5:00 pm.
5. Arrive	The bus always arrives on time.
6. Take	I never take tests.
7. Wake up	I wake up tv.
8. Go to bed	My mom goes to bed for me.
9. Depart	I depart by hello.
10. Succeed	I can succeed if I try.

Body Verbs

Directions in English: Write a New Sentence with a dictionary.
Directions in Chinese:写一个新的句子。
Directions in Spanish: Escribe una nueva oración creativa.
Directions in Korean: 새로운 창의적인 문장을 작성하시오.

Lie down

Get up

Go

Come

Arrive

Take

Wake up

Go to bed

Depart

Succeed

Body Verbs

Directions in English: Questions - Translate to Your Language
Directions in Chinese: 用您的语言翻译
Directions in Spanish: Traducir en su idioma
Directions in Korean: 한국어로 번역하십시오.

Lie down	**What time do you lie down?**
Get up	**When do you have to get up in the morning?**
Go	**Where are you going?**
Come	**When are you coming?**
Arrive	**What time does the bus arrive?**
Take	**Do you take lunch or buy one?**
Wake up	**When does she wake up?**
Go to bed	**Why does he go to bed?**
Depart	**When does the plane depart?**
Succeed	**How can I succeed more?**

Body Verbs

Directions in English: Write the questions from the previous page in English.
Directions in Chinese: 用英语写下上一页的问题。
Directions in Spanish: Escriba las preguntas de la página anterior en inglés.
Directions in Korean: 이전 페이지의 질문을 영어로 작성하십시오.

Lie down	
Get up	
Go	
Come	
Arrive	
Take	
Wake up	
Go to bed	
Depart	
Succeed	

81. Whole Body Verbs

In order to learn a language fast, you must learn many verbs to describe your thinking processes!

! 为了快速学习语言，你必须学习许多动词来描述你的大脑行为。

Para aprender el idioma rápidamente, debes aprender muchos verbos para describir tu comportamiento cerebral.

언어를 빨리 배우려면 사고 과정을 설명하는 동사를 많이 배워야합니다!

Chapter 9
How To Talk About Your Thoughts
如何谈论你的想法
Cómo Hablar Sobre Tus Pensamientos
당신의 생각에 대해 이야기하는 법

Brain Verbs

Acquisition of New Vocabulary
Directions in English: Write in Your Language
Directions in Chinese: 用中文写
Directions in Spanish: Escribe En Tu Idioma
Directions in Korea: 한글

Brain Verbs	
1. Think	
2. Decide	
3. Memorize	
4. Study	
5. Analyze	
6. Guess	
7. Ponder	
8. Reflect	
9. Consider	
10. Imagine	

Brain Verbs

Directions in English: Write 3 times
Directions in Chinese: 写3次
Directions in Spanish: Escribe en Ingles
Directions in Korean: 영어로 3 번 쓰기

1. **Think**

2. **Decide**

3. **Memorize**

4. **Study**

5. **Analyze**

6. **Guess**

7. **Ponder**

8. **Reflect**

9. **Consider**

10. **Imagine**

BRAIN VERBS	I	YOU	HE/SHE/IT	WE	THEY
Think	I think	You think	He or she thinks	We think	They think
Think					
Decide					
Memorize					
Study					
Analyze					
Guess					
Ponder					
Reflect					
Consider					
Succeed					

9c. Brain Verbs – Conjugations - Find the appropriate verb写下合适的动词。
Encuentra el verbo apropiado para el pronombre대명사에 적절한 동사를 찾
으십시오.

Brain Verbs

GUESS THE VOCABULARY WORD
Directions in English: Guess the vocabulary word.
Directions in Chinese: 猜猜这个单词。
Directions in Spanish: Intenta descifrar la palabra del vocabulario.
Directions in Korean: 단어를 알아내시오.

1. inkth

2. idedce

3. zemimore

4. yduts

5. ezylana

6. sseug

7. rednop

8. tcelfer

9. redisnoc

10. enigami

Brain Verbs

1. Think — You think too much!

2. Decide — I decide what is best for me.

3. Memorize — I can memorize many words.

4. Study — I study all of the time.

5. Analyze — He analyzes everything!

6. Guess — I guess this is goodbye!

7. Ponder — I ponder my decisions.

8. Reflect — I reflect before I speak.

9. Consider — I consider my budget first.

10. Imagine — I imagine myself as a star.

Brain verbs

Directions in English: Copy The Sentence from the previous page
Directions in Chinese: 写下句子。
Directions in Spanish: Escribe la oracEón de la página anterior.
Directions in Korean: 이전 페이지에서 배운 문장을 다시 작성하시오.

1. **Think**

2. **Decide**

3. **Memorize**

4. **Study**

5. **Analyze**

6. **Guess**

7. **Ponder**

8. **Reflect**

9. **Consider**

10. **Imagine**

Brain Verbs	Directions in English: Fill In The Sentence Directions in Chinese: 用模型句子中的正确单词填充句子。 Directions in Spanish: Completa la oración con las palabras correctas de las oraciones modelo. Directions in Korean: 문장을 완성하시오.
1. Think	You _____ too much!
2. Decide	I _____ what is best for me.
3. Memorize	I can _____ many words.
4. Study	I _____ all of the time.
5. Analyze	He _____ everything!
6. Guess	I _____ this is goodbye!
7. Ponder	I _____ my decisions.
8. Reflect	I _____ before I speak.
9. Consider	I _____ my budget first.
10. Imagine	I _____ myself as a star.

Brain Verbs	Directions in English: Fill In The Sentence Directions in Chinese: 用模型句子中的正确单词填充句子。 Directions in Spanish: Completa la oración con las palabras correctas de las oraciones modelo. Directions in Korean: 문장을 완성하시오.
1. Think	You think _____ _____!
2. Decide	I decide what is _____ ____ ___.
3. Memorize	I can memorize _____ _____.
4. Study	I study ____ ___ ____ _____.
5. Analyze	He analyzes _____!
6. Guess	I guess _____ __ _____!
7. Ponder	I ponder ____ _____.
8. Reflect	I reflect before _____ _____.
9. Consider	I consider ___ _____ _____.
10. Imagine	I imagine _____ __ __ _____.

Brain Verbs

Directions in English: True / False。Put T or F Below
Directions in Chinese: 在下面写正确或不正确 写T为正确或F 为不正确。
Directions in Spanish: Escribe T si es verdadero, F si es falso
Directions in Korean: 참이면 T / 거짓이면 F 를 적으시오

1. **Think** — **You never think.**

2. **Decide** — **I decide for everybody.**

3. **Memorize** — **No one can remember anything.**

4. **Study** — **I never study.**

5. **Analyze** — **My foot analyzes the problem.**

6. **Guess** — **I guess I know everything.**

7. **Ponder** — **It's not good to ponder a decision first.**

8. **Reflect** — **Before you leave, don't reflect on what to do in the United States.**

9. **Consider** — **I should consider my goals.**

10. **Imagine** — **Imagine yourself as a piece of grass.**

Brain Verbs

Directions in English: Write a New Sentence with a dictionary.
Directions in Chinese: 写一个新的句子。
Directions in Spanish: Escribe una nueva oración creativa.
Directions in Korean: 새로운 창의적인 문장을 작성하시오.

1. **Think**

2. **Decide**

3. **Memorize**

4. **Study**

5. **Analyze**

6. **Guess**

7. **Ponder**

8. **Reflect**

9. **Consider**

10. **Imagine**

Brain Verbs

Directions in English: Questions - Translate to Your Language
Directions in Chinese: 用您的语言翻译
Directions in Spanish: Traducir en su idioma
Directions in Korean: 한국어로 번역하십시오.

1. Think	What are you thinking about?
2. Decide	Who decides for you?
3. Memorize	Can you memorize it?
4. Study	Do you study every night?
5. Analyze	Can you analyze it?
6. Guess	Guess what?
7. Ponder	What do you ponder most?
8. Reflect	Do you reflect on your grades?
9. Consider	Can you consider others also?
10. Imagine	What do you imagine about the future?

Brain Verbs

Directions in English: Write the questions from the previous page in English.
Directions in Chinese: 用英语写下上一页的问题。
Directions in Spanish: Escriba las preguntas de la página anterior en inglés.
Directions in Korean: 이전 페이지의 질문을 영어로 작성하십시오.

1. Think

2. Decide

3. Memorize

4. Study

5. Analyze

6. Guess

7. Ponder

8. Reflect

9. Consider

10. Imagine

In order to learn a language fast, you must learn many verbs for the actions that you do with your head.

为了快速学习一门语言，你必须学习许多动词，你头脑的动作。

Para aprender un idioma rápido, debes aprender muchos verbos para las acciones que haces con tu cabeza.

언어를 빨리 배우려면 머리로하는 행동에 대한 여러 가지 동사를 배워야합니다.

Chapter 10
How To Talk About What You Do With Your Head
如何谈论你在做什么
Cómo hablar sobre lo que haces con tu cabeza
당신이 당신의 머리로하는 일 에 대해 이야기하는 법

Head Verbs

1. Nod	
2. Shake	
3. Turn	
4. Look up	
5. Adjust	
6. Put up	
7. Rotate	
8. Move	
9. Bend	
10. Raise up	

Head Verbs

Directions in English: Write 3 times
Directions in Chinese: 写3次
Directions in Spanish: Escribe en Ingles
Directions in Korean: 영어로 3 번 쓰기

1. Nod

2. Shake

3. Turn

4. Look up

5. Adjust

6. Put up

7. Rotate

8. Move

9. Bend

10. Raise up

Head Verbs

GUESS THE VOCABULARY WORD
Directions in English: Guess the vocabulary word.
Directions in Chinese: 猜猜这个单词。
Directions in Spanish: Intenta descifrar la palabra del vocabulario.
Directions in Korean: 단어를 알아내시오.

1. don

2. ekahs

3. nrut

4. pu kool

5. tsujda

6. pu tup

7. etator

8. evom

9. dneb

10. pu esiar

HEAD VERBS	I	YOU	HE/ SHE/IT	WE	THEY
Nod	I eat	You eat	He or she eats	We eat	They eat
Nod					
Shake					
Look up					
Adjust					
Put up					
Rotate					
Move					
Bend					
Raise up					
Turn					

10d. Whole Body Verbs – Conjugations - Find the appropriate verb写下合适的动词。 **Encuentra el verbo apropiado para el pronombre**대명사에 적절한 동사를 찾으십시오.

153

Head Verbs	Directions in English: Underline The Verb Directions in Chinese: 强调动词。 Directions in Spanish: Subraya el verbo. Directions in Korean: 동사에 밑줄 치시오.
1. Nod	She nods yes to the bus driver.
2. Shake	I shake my head no.
3. Turn	I turned to see the car.
4. Look up	Look up and imagine your life.
5. Adjust	Adjust your head to the right.
6. Put up	Put up your heads, please.
7. Rotate	Rotate from left to right.
8. Move	Move your head.
9. Bend	Bend your head forward.
10. Raise up	Raise up your head.

Head Verbs

Directions in English: Copy The Sentence from the previous page
Directions in Chinese: 写下句子。
Directions in Spanish: Escribe la oracEón de la página anterior.
Directions in Korean: 이전 페이지에서 배운 문장을 다시 작성하시오.

1. **Nod**

2. **Shake**

3. **Turn**

4. **Look up**

5. **Adjust**

6. **Put up**

7. **Rotate**

8. **Move**

9. **Bend**

10. **Raise up**

Head Verbs

1. Nod   She _____ yes to the bus driver.

2. Shake   I _____ my head no.

3. Turn   I _____ to see the car.

4. Look up   _____ ___ and imagine your life.

5. Adjust   _____ your head to the right.

6. Put up   _____ _____ your heads, please.

7. Rotate   _____ from left to right.

8. Move   _____ your head.

9. Bend   _____ your head forward.

10. Raise up   _____ _____ your head.

Head Verbs

Directions in English: Fill In The Sentence
Directions in Chinese: 用模型句子中的正确单词填充句子。
Directions in Spanish: Completa la oración con las palabras correctas de las oraciones modelo.
Directions in Korean: 문장을 완성하시오.

1. **Nod** She nods yes ___ ____ ____ _____.

2. **Shake** I shake ____ _____ ___.

3. **Turn** I turned ___ ___ ___ ____.

4. **Look up** Look up and imagine ____ _____.

5. **Adjust** Adjust your head ___ _____ _____.

6. **Put up** Put up _____ _____, please.

7. **Rotate** Rotate from left ____ _____.

8. **Move** Move your _____.

9. **Bend** Bend your head _____.

10. **Raise up** Raise up your _____.

10h. Head Verbs   **157**

Head Verbs

Directions in English: True / False。Put T or F Below
Directions in Chinese: 在下面写正确或不正确 写T为正确或F为不正确。
Directions in Spanish: Escribe T si es verdadero, F si es falso
Directions in Korean: 참이면 T / 거짓이면 F 를 적으시오

1. Nod	She nods to the tree.
2. Shake	I shake my head okay.
3. Turn	I turned to tv..
4. Look up	Look up and see the dust.
5. Adjust	Adjust your head to the table.
6. Put up	Put up your heads on your feet.
7. Rotate	Rotate from left to beach.
8. Move	Move your head a little.
9. Bend	Bend your head food.
10. Raise up	Raise up your heads, dolls.

Head Verbs

1. Nod

2. Shake

3. Turn

4. Look up

5. Adjust

6. Put up

7. Rotate

8. Move

9. Bend

10. Raise up

Head verbs

Directions in English: Questions - Translate to Your Language
Directions in Chinese: 用您的语言翻译
Directions in Spanish: Traducir en su idioma
Directions in Korean: 한국어로 번역하십시오.

1. Nod	Can you nod your head yes or no?
2. Shake	Why are you shaking your head?
3. Turn	Can you turn your head?
4. Look up	Could you look up, please?
5. Adjust	Could you adjust your head?
6. Put up	Could you put up your heads?
7. Rotate	Who can rotate his or her head?
8. Move	Can you move your head?
9. Bend	Could you bend your head forward?
10. Raise up	Could everyone raise up your heads, please?

Head Verbs

Directions in English: Write the questions from the previous page in English.
Directions in Chinese: 用英文写上一页的问题。
Directions in Spanish: Escriba las preguntas de la página anterior en inglés.
Directions in Korean: 이전 페이지의 질문을 영어로 작성하십시오.

1. Nod

2. Shake

3. Turn

4. Look up

5. Adjust

6. Put up

7. Rotate

8. Move

9. Bend

10. Raise up

In order to learn a language fast, you must learn many verbs for the actions you do with your eyes!

为了快速学习一门语言，你必须学习许多动词，比如你用眼睛做的动作。

¡Para aprender un idioma rápido, debes aprender muchos verbos para las acciones que haces con tus ojos!

언어를 빨리 배우려면 눈으로하는 행동에 대한 여러 동사를 배워야합니다!

Chapter 11
How To Talk About What You See
如何谈论你所看到的
Cómo Hablar Sobre Lo Que Ves
당신이 보는 것에 대해 이야기 하는 법

Eye Verbs

	Acquisition of New Vocabulary **Directions in English: Write in Your Language** **Directions in Chinese:**用中文写 **Directions in Spanish: Escribe En Tu Idioma** **Directions in Korea:** 한글
1. Look	
2. See	
3. Open	
4. Stare	
5. Glare	
6. Wink	
7. Cry	
8. Read	
9. Focus	
10. Watch	

Eye Verbs

Directions in English: Write 3 times
Directions in Chinese: 写3次
Directions in Spanish: Escribe en Ingles
Directions in Korean: 영어로 3 번 쓰기

1. Look	
2. See	
3. Open	
4. Stare	
5. Glare	
6. Wink	
7. Cry	
8. Read	
9. Focus	
10. Watch	

Eye Verbs

GUESS THE VOCABULARY WORD
Directions in English: Guess the vocabulary word.
Directions in Chinese: 猜猜这个单词。
Directions in Spanish: Intenta descifrar la palabra del vocabulario.
Directions in Korean: 단어를 알아내시오.

1. kool

2. ees

3. nepo

4. erats

5. eralg

6. kniw

7. yrc

8. daer

9. sucof

10. chwat

EYE VERBS	I	YOU	HE/SHE/IT	WE	THEY
Look	I look	You look	He or she looks	We look	They look
Look					
See					
Open					
Stare					
Glare					
Wink					
Cry					
Read					
Focus					
Watch					

11e. Eye Verbs – Conjugations - Find the appropriate verb写下合适的动词。 Encuentra el verbo apropiado para el pronombre대명사에 적절한 동사를 찾으십시오.

166

Eye Verbs	Directions in English: Underline The Verb Directions in Chinese: 强调动词。 Directions in Spanish: Subraya el verbo. Directions in Korean: 동사에 밑줄 치시오.
1. Look	Look at my face.
2. See	I see so many new faces.
3. Open	Open your books to page 59.
4. Stare	Don't stare; it's not polite!
5. Glare	He glared because he was angry.
6. Wink	The boy winked at his father.
7. Cry	They cried when they heard the party was off.
8. Read	She reads one book a week.
9. Focus	Try to focus on what you are doing.
10. Watch	Watch out for strangers.

Eye Verbs

Directions in English: Copy The Sentence from the previous page
Directions in Chinese: 写下句子。
Directions in Spanish: Escribe la oración de la página anterior.
Directions in Korean: 이전 페이지에서 배운 문장을 다시 작성하시오.

1. Look

2. See

3. Open

4. Stare

5. Glare

6. Wink

7. Cry

8. Read

9. Focus

10. Watch

Eye Verbs

1. **Look** — Look _____ _____ face.

2. **See** — I see so many _____ _____.

3. **Open** — Open your books __ _____ ___.

4. **Stare** — Don't stare; it's not _____!

5. **Glare** — He glared because he ____ _____.

6. **Wink** — The boy winked at his _____.

7. **Cry** — They cried when they heard the _____ _____ _____.

8. **Read** — She reads one book __ _____.

9. **Focus** — Try to focus ____ _____ ____ _____.

10. **Watch** — Watch out _____ _____.

Eye Verbs	**Sentence Completion** **Directions in English: Fill In The Sentence** **Directions in Chinese:** 用模型句子中的正确单词填充句子。 **Directions in Spanish: Completa la oración con las palabras** **correctas de las oraciones modelo.** **Directions in Korean:** 문장을 완성하시오.
1. Look	_____ at my face.
2. See	I _____ so many new faces.
3. Open	_____ your books to page 59.
4. Stare	Don't _____; it's not polite!
5. Glare	He _____ because he is angry.
6. Wink	The boy _____ at his father.
7. Cry	They _____ when get too tired.
8. Read	She _____ one book a week.
9. Focus	Try to _____ on what you are doing.
10. Watch	_____ out for strangers.

Eye Verbs	Assessment/Error Detection Directions in English: True / False ∘ Put T or F Below Directions in Chinese: 在下面写正确或不正确 写T为正确或F为不正确。 Directions in Spanish: Escribe T si es verdadero, F si es falso Directions in Korean: 참이면 **T** / 거짓이면 **F** 를 적으시오
1. Look	Look at my heart.
2. See	I see so many bugs.
3. Open	Open your wallet and give me all of your money.
4. Stare	It's good to not stare at people!
5. Glare	Glare means to like someone.
6. Wink	Wink at strangers.
7. Cry	Cry if you're hungry.
8. Read	Read books often.
9. Focus	Focus on other people's gossip.
10. Watch	Watch the bathroom.

Eye Verbs

Directions in English: Write a New Sentence with a dictionary.
Directions in Chinese: 写一个新的句子。
Directions in Spanish: Escribe una nueva oración creativa.
Directions in Korean: 새로운 창의적인 문장을 작성하시오.

1. Look

2. See

3. Open

4. Stare

5. Glare

6. Wink

7. Cry

8. Read

9. Focus

10. Watch

Eye Verbs

Directions in English: Questions - Translate to Your Language
Directions in Chinese: 用您的语言翻译
Directions in Spanish: Traducir en su idioma
Directions in Korean: 한국어로 번역하십시오.

1. Look	Why are you looking that way?
2. See	What do you see?
3. Open	Can I open my eyes now?
4. Stare	Why are you staring?
5. Glare	Do you glare at everyone?
6. Wink	Who are you winking at?
7. Cry	Why are you crying?
8. Read	Where do we begin to read?
9. Focus	Are you focusing?
10. Watch	Are you watching closely?

Eye Verbs

Directions in English: Write the questions from the previous page in English.
Directions in Chinese: 用英语写下上一页的问题。
Directions in Spanish: Escriba las preguntas de la página anterior en inglés.
Directions in Korean: 이전 페이지의 질문을 영어로 작성하십시오.

1. Look

2. See

3. Open

4. Stare

5. Glare

6. Wink

7. Cry

8. Read

9. Focus

10. Watch

In order to learn a language fast, you must learn many verbs for the actions you do with your mouth!

为了快速学习语言，你必须学习许多动词，你用你的嘴做的动作！

¡Para aprender un idioma rápido, debes aprender muchos verbos para las acciones que haces con tu boca!

언어를 빨리 배우려면 입으로하는 행동에 대한 여러 동사를 배워야합니다!

Chapter 12
How To Talk About What You Say
如何谈论你说的话
Cómo Hablar Sobre Lo Que Dices
당신이 말하는 것에 대해 이야기하는 법

Mouth Verbs

Acquisition of New Vocabulary
Directions in English: Write in Your Language
Directions in Chinese:用中文写
Directions in Spanish: Escribe En Tu Idioma
Directions in Korea: 한글

1. Eat	
2. Speak	
3. Say	
4. Talk	
5. Ask	
6. Tell	
7. Shout	
8. Pray	
9. Kiss	
10. Taste	

Mouth Verbs

Directions in English: Write 3 times
Directions in Chinese: 写3次
Directions in Spanish: Escribe en Ingles
Directions in Korean: 영어로 3 번 쓰기

1. Eat

2. Speak

3. Say

4. Talk

5. Ask

6. Tell

7. Shout

8. Pray

9. Kiss

10. Taste

Mouth Verbs

GUESS THE VOCABULARY WORD
Directions in English: Guess the vocabulary word.
Directions in Chinese: 猜猜这个单词。
Directions in Spanish: Intenta descifrar la palabra del vocabulario.
Directions in Korean: 단어를 알아내시오.

1. tae

2. kaeps

3. yas

4. klat

5. ksa

6. llet

7. tuoch

8. yarp

9. ssik

10. etast

MOUTH VERBS	I	YOU	HE/SHE/IT	WE	THEY
Eat	I eat	You eat	He or she eats	We eat	They eat
Eat					
Speak					
Say					
Talk					
Ask					
Tell					
Shout					
Pray					
Kiss					
Taste					

12d. Mouth Verbs – Conjugations - Find the appropriate verb写下合适的动词。 Encuentra el verbo apropiado para el pronombre대명사에 적절한 동사를 찾으십시오.

Mouth Verbs

Directions in English: Underline The Verb
Directions in Chinese: 强调动词。
Directions in Spanish: Subraya el verbo.
Directions in Korean: 동사에 밑줄 치시오.

1. Eat	I eat a big breakfast in the morning.
2. Speak	I always speak to my parents.
3. Say	She said, "Hello!"
4. Talk	Let's talk about your grades.
5. Ask	Always ask questions if you don't understand.
6. Tell	If you feel uncomfortable, tell someone about it.
7. Shout	Don't shout, just talk.
8. Pray	Pray for good weather.
9. Kiss	The frog kissed the princess.
10. Taste	It tastes like coffee.

Mouth Verbs

Directions in English: Copy The Sentence from the previous page
Directions in Chinese: 写下句子。
Directions in Spanish: Escribe la oración de la página anterior.
Directions in Korean: 이전 페이지에서 배운 문장을 다시 작성하시오.

1. **Eat**

2. **Speak**

3. **Say**

4. **Talk**

5. **Ask**

6. **Tell**

7. **Shout**

8. **Pray**

9. **Kiss**

10. **Taste**

Mouth Verbs

Directions in English: Fill In The Sentence
Directions in Chinese: 用模型句子中的正确单词填充句子。
Directions in Spanish: Completa la oración con las palabras correctas de las oraciones modelo.
Directions in Korean: 문장을 완성하시오.

1. Eat   I _____ a big breakfast in the morning.

2. Speak   I always _____ to my parents.

3. Say   She _____, "Hello!"

4. Talk   Let's _____ about your grades.

5. Ask   Always _____ questions if you don't understand.

6. Tell   If you feel uncomfortable, _____ someone about it.

7. Shout   Don't _____, just talk.

8. Pray   _____ for good weather.

9. Kiss   The frog _____ the princess.

10. Taste   It _____ like coffee.

Mouth Verbs

Directions in English: Fill In The Sentence
Directions in Chinese: 用模型句子中的正确单词填充句子。
Directions in Spanish: Completa la oración con las palabras correctas de las oraciones modelo.
Directions in Korean: 문장을 완성하시오.

1. **Eat** I eat a big breakfast in the _____.

2. **Speak** I always speak to _____ _____.

3. **Say** She says, _____

4. **Talk** Let's _____ about your grades.

5. **Ask** Always _____questions if you don't understand.

6. **Tell** If you feel uncomfortable, tell _____about it.

7. **Shout** Don't shout, _____ _____.

8. **Pray** Pray for good _____.

9. **Kiss** The frog kisses _____ _____.

10. **Taste** It tastes like _____.

Mouth Verbs	Directions in English: True / False · Put T or F Below Directions in Chinese: 在下面写正确或不正确 写T为正确或 F为不正确。 Directions in Spanish: Escribe T si es verdadero, F si es falso Directions in Korean: 참이면 T / 거짓이면 F 를 적으시오
1. Eat	I eat a big breakfast in the pigsty.
2. Speak	I always speak to house.
3. Say	I can understand what you say.
4. Talk	Talk is more important than actions.
5. Ask	Ask before you take.
6. Tell	Tell on other people.
7. Shout	Don't shout, just talk.
8. Pray	Pray to the water.
9. Kiss	The frog kissed the princess.
10. Taste	Coffee tastes like apples.

Mouth Verbs

Directions in English: Write a New Sentence with a dictionary.
Directions in Chinese:写一个新的句子。
Directions in Spanish: Escribe una nueva oración creativa.
Directions in Korean: 새로운 창의적인 문장을 작성하시오.

1. Eat

2. Speak

3. Say

4. Talk

5. Ask

6. Tell

7. Shout

8. Pray

9. Kiss

10. Taste

Mouth Verbs

Directions in English: Questions - Translate to Your Language
Directions in Chinese: 用您的语言翻译
Directions in Spanish: Traducir en su idioma
Directions in Korean: 한국어로 번역하십시오.

1. Eat — What do you like to eat?

2. Speak — Can you speak up?

3. Say — What did you say?

4. Talk — Can I talk to you?

5. Ask — Do you want to ask a question?

6. Tell — What can you tell us about this?

7. Shout — Why are you shouting?

8. Pray — Do you ever pray?

9. Kiss — Can you give me a kiss?

10. Taste — How does it taste?

Mouth Verbs

Directions in English: Write the questions from the previous page in English.
Directions in Chinese: 用英语写下上一页的问题。
Directions in Spanish: Escriba las preguntas de la página anterior en inglés.
Directions in Korean: 이전 페이지의 질문을 영어로 작성하십시오.

1. Eat

2. Speak

3. Say

4. Talk

5. Ask

6. Tell

7. Shout

8. Pray

9. Kiss

10. Taste

In order to learn a language fast, you must learn many verbs for the actions you do with your ears!

为了快速学习一门语言，你必须学习许多动词，以便你用耳朵进行的动作！

¡Para aprender un idioma rápido, debes aprender muchos verbos para las acciones que haces con tus oídos!

당신이 들은 것을 말하는 법

Chapter 13
How To Talk About What You Hear
如何谈论你听到的东西
Cómo Hablar Sobre Lo Que Oyes
어떻게 듣는지 이야기하는 법

Ear Verbs	Acquisition of New Vocabulary Directions in English: Write in Your Language Directions in Chinese:用中文写 Directions in Spanish: Escribe En Tu Idioma Directions in Korea: 한글
1. Hear	
2. Listen	
3. Perceive	
4. Recognize	
5. Distinguish	
6. Discern	
7. Tap into	
8. Pick up on	
9. Hearken	
10. Heed	

Ear Verbs

Directions in English: Write 3 times
Directions in Chinese: 写3次
Directions in Spanish: Escribe en Ingles
Directions in Korean: 영어로 3 번 쓰기

1. **Hear**

2. **Listen**

3. **Perceive**

4. **Recognize**

5. **Distinguish**

6. **Discern**

7. **Tap into**

8. **Pick up on**

9. **Hearken**

10. **Heed**

Ear Verbs

GUESS THE VOCABULARY WORD
Directions in English: Guess the vocabulary word.
Directions in Chinese: 猜猜这个单词。
Directions in Spanish: Intenta descifrar la palabra del vocabulario.
Directions in Korean: 단어를 알아내시오.

1. raeh

2. netsil

3. eveicrep

4. ezingocer

5. hsiugnitsid

6. nrecsid

7. Pat otni

8. No pu kcip

9. nekraeh

10. deeh

EAR VERBS	I	YOU	HE/SHE/IT	WE	THEY
Hear	I hear	You hear	He or she hears	We hear	They hear
Hear					
Listen					
Perceive					
Recognize					
Distinguish					
Discern					
Tap into					
Pick up on					
Hearken					
Heed					

13f. Ear Verbs – Conjugations - Find the appropriate verb写下合适的动词。
Encuentra el verbo apropiado para el pronombre대명사에 적절한 동사
를 찾으십시오.

Ear Verbs	Directions in English: Underline The Verb Directions in Chinese: 强调动词。 Directions in Spanish: Subraya el verbo. Directions in Korean: 동사에 밑줄 치시오.
1. Hear	I hear noises in your room.
2. Listen	Listen carefully to the teacher.
3. Perceive	He perceived that he was not alone.
4. Recognize	You can recognize hip hop music.
5. Distinguish	I distinguished a baby's sound.
6. Discern	The postman discerned that no one was home after he knocked.
8. Pick up on	I could pick up on your light footsteps.
9. Hearken	The student who hearkens, gets As.
10. Heed	You should heed your parents advice.

Ear Verbs

Directions in English: Copy The Sentence from the previous page
Directions in Chinese: 写下句子。
Directions in Spanish: Escribe la oracEón de la página anterior.
Directions in Korean: 이전 페이지에서 배운 문장을 다시 작성하시오.

1. Hear

2. Listen

3. Perceive

4. Recognize

5. Distinguish

6. Discern

7. Tap into

8. Pick up on

9. Hearken

10. Heed

Ear Verbs	Directions in English: Fill In The Sentence Directions in Chinese: 用模型句子中的正确单词填充句子。 Directions in Spanish: Completa la oración con las palabras correctas de las oraciones modelo. Directions in Korean: 문장을 완성하시오.
1. Hear	I _____ noises in your room.
2. Listen	_____ carefully to the teacher.
3. Perceive	He _____ that he was not serious.
4. Recognize	You can _____ hip hop music.
5. Distinguish	I _____ a baby's sound.
6. Discern	The postman _____ that no one was home after he knocked.
8. Pick up on	I could _____ your light footsteps.
9. Hearken	The student who _____, gets As.
10. Heed	You should _____ your parents advice.

Ear Verbs	Directions in English: Fill In The Sentence Directions in Chinese: 用模型句子中的正确单词填充句子。 Directions in Spanish: Completa la oración con las palabras correctas de las oraciones modelo. Directions in Korean: 문장을 완성하시오.
1. hear	I hear noises in your room.
2. listen	Listen carefully to the teacher.
3. perceive	He perceived that he was not serious.
4. recognize	You can recognize hip hop music.
5. distinguish	I distinguished a baby's sound.
6. discern	The postman discerned that no one was home after he knocked.
8. Pick up on	I could pick up on your light footsteps.
9. hearken	The student who hearkens, gets As.
10. heed	You should heed your parents advice.

Ear Verbs	**Directions in English:** True / False ∘ Put T or F Below **Directions in Chinese:** 在下面写正确或不正确 写T为正确或F为不正确。 **Directions in Spanish:** Escribe T si es verdadero, F si es falso **Directions in Korean:** 참이면 T / 거짓이면 F 를 적으시오
1. Hear	I hear eyes in your room.
2. Listen	Listen carefully to the cup.
3. Perceive	You can perceive a person is nice by the tone of voice.
4. Recognize	You can recognize hip hop music when you hear it.
5. Distinguish	I can distinguish a dog's bark.
6. Discern	The postman discerned that apple pie was home.
8. Pick up on	You can pick up on your roommate's voice.
9. Hearken	The student who hearkens, gets fails.
10. Heed	You should heed your parents' advice.

Ear Verbs	Directions in English: Write a New Sentence with a dictionary. Directions in Chinese:写一个新的句子。 Directions in Spanish: Escribe una nueva oración creativa. Directions in Korean: 새로운 창의적인 문장을 작성하시오.
1. Hear	
2. Listen	
3. Perceive	
4. Recognize	
5. Distinguish	
6. Discern	
7. Tap into	
8. Pick up on	
9. Hearken	
10. Heed	

Ear Verbs	Directions in English: Questions - Translate to Your Language Directions in Chinese: 用您的语言翻译 Directions in Spanish: Traducir en su idioma Directions in Korean: 한국어로 번역하십시오.
1. Hear	What do you hear?
2. Listen	Do you want to listen along?
3. Perceive	What sound do you perceive?
4. Recognize	What voice do you recognize?
5. Distinguish	Can you distinguish the music types?
6. Discern	Whose name did you discern?
7. Tap into	Where did you tap into that band?
8. Pick up on	How did you pick up on it?
9. Hearken	Do you hearken to your teachers?
10. Heed	Do you heed your parents.

Ear Verbs	Directions in English: Write the questions from the previous page in English. Directions in Chinese:用英语写下上一页的问题。 Directions in Spanish: Escriba las preguntas de la página anterior en inglés. Directions in Korean: 이전 페이지의 질문을 영어로 작성하십시오.
1. Hear	
2. Listen	
3. Perceive	
4. Recognize	
5. Distinguish	
6. Discern	
7. Tap into	
8. Pick up on	
9. Hearken	
10. Heed	

In order to learn a language fast, you must learn many verbs for the actions you do with your hands!

为了快速学习一门语言，你必须学习许多动作，你用手做的动作！

¡Para aprender un idioma rápido, debes aprender muchos verbos para las acciones que haces con tus manos!

언어를 빨리 배우려면 손으로하는 행동에 대한 여러 동사를 배워야합니다!

Chapter 14
How To Talk About What You Do
如何谈论你做什么
Cómo Hablar Sobre Lo Que Haces
당신이하는 일에 대해 이야기 하는 법

Hand Verbs

1. Shake

2. Give

3. Feel

4. Hold

5. Write

6. Play

7. Handle

8. Wash

9. Wave

10. Clap

Hand Verbs

Directions in English: Write 3 times
Directions in Chinese: 写3次
Directions in Spanish: Escribe en Ingles
Directions in Korean: 영어로 3 번 쓰기

1. Shake

2. Give

3. Feel

4. Hold

5. Write

6. Play

7. Handle

8. Wash

9. Wave

10. Clap

Hand Verbs

GUESS THE VOCABULARY WORD
Directions in English: Guess the vocabulary word.
Directions in Chinese: 猜猜这个单词。
Directions in Spanish: Intenta descifrar la palabra del vocabulario.
Directions in Korean: 단어를 알아내시오.

1. ekahs

2. evig

3. leef

4. dloh

5. etirw

6. yalp

7. eldnah

8. hsaw

9. evaw

10. palc

HAND VERBS	I	YOU	HE/SHE/IT	WE	THEY
Shake	I shake	You shake	He or she shakes	We shake	They shake
Shake					
Give					
Feel					
Hold					
Write					
Play					
Handle					
Wash					
Wave					
Clap					

14d. Whole Body Verbs – Conjugations - Find the appropriate verb写下合适的动词。 **Encuentra el verbo apropiado para el pronombre**대명사에 적절한 동사를 찾으십시오.

Hand Verbs

Directions in English: Underline The Verb
Directions in Chinese: 强调动词。
Directions in Spanish: Subraya el verbo.
Directions in Korean: 동사에 밑줄 치시오.

1. Shake	The mayor shakes hands a lot.
2. Give	Give to the poor and hurt.
3. Feel	You can feel the softness.
4. Hold	Hold hands with your classmate.
5. Write	He writes home once a week.
6. Play	The man plays games at his job.
7. Handle	They handle all lunches for us.
8. Wash	Wash your hands before you eat.
9. Wave	Don't wave at a bear.
10. Clap	Hold the clapping until the end.

Hand Verbs

Directions in English: Copy The Sentence from the previous page
Directions in Chinese: 写下句子。
Directions in Spanish: Escribe la oracEón de la página anterior.
Directions in Korean: 이전 페이지에서 배운 문장을 다시 작성하시오.

1. Shake

2. Give

3. Feel

4. Hold

5. Write

6. Play

7. Handle

8. Wash

9. Wave

10. Clap

Hand Verbs

1. **Shake**   The mayor _____ hands a lot.

2. **Give**   _____ to the poor and hurt.

3. **Feel**   You can _____ the softness.

4. **Hold**   _____ hands with your classmate.

5. **Write**   He _____ home once a week.

6. **Play**   The man _____ games at his job.

7. **Handle**   They _____ all lunches for us.

8. **Wash**   _____ your hands before you eat.

9. **Wave**   Don't _____ at a bear.

10. **Clap**   Hold the _____ for the end.

14g. Hand Verbs   **208**

Hand Verbs

Directions in English: Fill In The Sentence
Directions in Chinese: 用模型句子中的正确单词填充句子。
Directions in Spanish: Completa la oración con las palabras correctas de las oraciones modelo.
Directions in Korean: 문장을 완성하시오.

1. **Shake**   The mayor shakes _____ a lot.

2. **Give**   Give to the _____ and hurt.

3. **Feel**   You can feel _____ _____.

4. **Hold**   Hold hands with _____ classmate.

5. **Write**   He writes home once ____ _____.

6. **Play**   The man plays _____ at his job.

7. **Handle**   They handle all _____ for us.

8. **Wash**   Wash your _____ before you eat.

9. **Wave**   Don't wave _____ ____ _____.

10. **Clap**   Hold the clapping for ____ _____.

14h. Hand Verbs

209

Hand Verbs	
1. Shake	The mayor shakes hands a lot.
2. Give	Give to the rich and famous.
3. Feel	Your hand can feel the solar system.
4. Hold	Hold hands with a lizard.
5. Write	He writes home too much.
6. Play	Everyone should play guitars.
7. Handle	You should handle your own lunch.
8. Wash	Wash your mouth before you eat.
9. Wave	Wave at the police.
10. Clap	Clap for the singing bear.

Hand Verbs

Directions in English: Write a New Sentence with a dictionary.
Directions in Chinese: 写一个新的句子。
Directions in Spanish: Escribe una nueva oración creativa.
Directions in Korean: 새로운 창의적인 문장을 작성하시오.

1. Shake

2. Give

3. Feel

4. Hold

5. Write

6. Play

7. Handle

8. Wash

9. Wave

10. Clap

Hand Verbs

Directions in English: Questions - Translate to Your Language
Directions in Chinese: 用您的语言翻译
Directions in Spanish: Traducir en su idioma
Directions in Korean: 한국어로 번역하십시오.

1. Shake	Why do the men shake hands?
2. Give	Can you give me a hand?
3. Feel	What does it feel like?
4. Hold	Can you hold it for me, please?
5. Write	Do you write home often?
6. Play	What are you playing?
7. Handle	Can you handle it yourself?
8. Wash	Did you wash your hands?
9. Wave	Who are you waving at?
10. Clap	Who claps the loudest?

Hand Verbs

Directions in English: Write the questions from the previous page in English.
Directions in Chinese:用英语写下上一页的问题。
Directions in Spanish: Escriba las preguntas de la página anterior en inglés.
Directions in Korean: 이전 페이지의 질문을 영어로 작성하십시오.

1. Shake

2. Give

3. Feel

4. Hold

5. Write

6. Play

7. Handle

8. Wash

9. Wave

10. Clap

In order to learn a language fast, you must learn many verbs for the actions of your heart!

为了快速学习一门语言，你必须学习许多动词来表达你内心的动作！

¡Para aprender un idioma rápido, debes aprender muchos verbos para las acciones de tu corazón!

언어를 빨리 배우기 위해서, 당신은 마음속에서 일어나는 일들에 관한 동사를 반드시 배워야 합니다.

Chapter 15
How To Talk About How You Feel
如何谈论你的感受
Cómo Hablar Sobre Cómo Te Sientes
당신이 어떻게 느끼는지를 표현하는 방법

Heart Verbs

Acquisition of New Vocabulary
Directions in English: Write in Your Language
Directions in Chinese: 用中文写
Directions in Spanish: Escribe En Tu Idioma
Directions in Korea: 한글

1. Love

2. Hate

3. Like

4. Dislike

5. Trust

6. Adore

7. Detest

8. Praise

9. Feel

10. Worship

Heart Verbs

Directions in English: Write 3 times
Directions in Chinese: 写3次
Directions in Spanish: Escribe en Ingles
Directions in Korean: 영어로 3 번 쓰기

1. **Love**

2. **Hate**

3. **Like**

4. **Dislike**

5. **Trust**

6. **Adore**

7. **Detest**

8. **Praise**

9. **Feel**

10. **Worship**

Heart Verbs

GUESS THE VOCABULARY WORD
Directions in English: Guess the vocabulary word.
Directions in Chinese: 猜猜这个单词。
Directions in Spanish: Intenta descifrar la palabra del vocabulario.
Directions in Korean: 단어를 알아내시오.

1. evol

2. etah

3. ekil

4. ekildis

5. usttr

6. eroda

7. tstede

8. esairp

9. leef

10. pihsrow

HEART VERBS	I	YOU	HE/SHE/IT	WE	THEY
Love	I love	You love	He or she loves	We love	They love
Love					
Hate					
Like					
Dislike					
Trust					
Adore					
Detest					
Praise					
Feel					
Worship					

15d. Whole Body Verbs – Conjugations - Find the appropriate verb写下合适的动词。 **Encuentra el verbo apropiado para el pronombre**대명사에 적절한 동사를 찾으십시오.

Heart Verbs

1. **Love** — I love chocolate chip cookies.

2. **Hate** — I hate to wash a dog.

3. **Like** — We like people who are friendly.

4. **Dislike** — We dislike the smell of trash.

5. **Trust** — We trust our best friends.

6. **Adore** — Children adore games and prizes.

7. **Detest** — Most people detest very hot food.

8. **Praise** — Praise and reward the hero.

9. **Feel** — I feel like I know you.

10. **Worship** — Worship movie stars.

Heart Verbs

Directions in English: Copy The Sentence from the previous page
Directions in Chinese: 写下句子。
Directions in Spanish: Escribe la oracEón de la página anterior.
Directions in Korean: 이전 페이지에서 배운 문장을 다시 작성하시오.

1. Love

2. Hate

3. Like

4. Dislike

5. Trust

6. Adore

7. Detest

8. Praise

9. Feel

10. Worship

Heart Verbs

1. **Love** I _____ chocolate chip cookies.

2. **Hate** I _____ to wash a dog.

3. **Like** We _____ people who like us.

4. **Dislike** We _____ the smell of trash.

5. **Trust** We _____ our best friends.

6. **Adore** Children _____ games.

7. **Detest** Most people _____ very hot food.

8. **Praise** _____ and reward the hero.

9. **Feel** I _____ like I know you.

10. **Worship** _____ and serve the best one.

Heart Verbs

1. **Love** — I _____ chocolate chip cookies.

2. **Hate** — I _____ to wash a dog.

3. **Like** — We _____ people who like us.

4. **Dislike** — We _____ the smell of trash.

5. **Trust** — We _____ our best friends.

6. **Adore** — Children _____ games.

7. **Detest** — Most people _____ very hot food.

8. **Praise** — _____ and reward the hero.

9. **Feel** — I _____ like I know you.

10. **Worship** — _____ and serve the best one.

Heart Verbs

Directions in English: True / False 。 Put T or F Below
Directions in Chinese: 在下面写正确或不正确 写T为正确或F为不正确。
Directions in Spanish: Escribe T si es verdadero, F si es falso
Directions in Korean: 참이면 T / 거짓이면 F 를 적으시오

1.	Love	I love chocolate chip cookies.
2.	Hate	Everyone hates very hot weather.
3.	Like	We like to eat grass.
4.	Dislike	We dislike the smell of trash.
5.	Trust	We trust our best friends.
6.	Adore	Children adore hot spices.
7.	Detest	Most people detest waiting for the bus.
8.	Praise	Praise and reward the hero.
9.	Feel	I feel excited at Disneyland.
10.	Worship	Worship movie stars.

223

Heart Verbs

Directions in English: Write a New Sentence with a dictionary.
Directions in Chinese:写一个新的句子。
Directions in Spanish: Escribe una nueva oración creativa.
Directions in Korean: 새로운 창의적인 문장을 작성하시오.

1. Love

2. Hate

3. Like

4. Dislike

5. Trust

6. Adore

7. Detest

8. Praise

9. Feel

10. Worship

Heart Verbs

Directions in English: Questions - Translate to Your Language
Directions in Chinese: 用您的语言翻译
Directions in Spanish: Traducir en su idioma
Directions in Korean: 한국어로 번역하십시오.

1. **Love** — Do I love chocolate?

2. **Hate** — Who hates dogs?

3. **Like** — Why do you like them?

4. **Dislike** — Why do you dislike each other?

5. **Trust** — What kind of person can you trust?

6. **Adore** — Do you adore children?

7. **Detest** — Why do they detest the food?

8. **Praise** — Why do you praise him?

9. **Feel** — How do you feel about it?

10. **Worship** — Who or what do you worship?

Heart Verbs

Directions in English: Write the questions from the previous page in English.
Directions in Chinese:用英语写下上一页的问题。
Directions in Spanish: Escriba las preguntas de la página anterior en inglés.
Directions in Korean: 이전 페이지의 질문을 영어로 작성하십시오.

1. Love

2. Hate

3. Like

4. Dislike

5. Trust

6. Adore

7. Detest

8. Praise

9. Feel

10. Worship

15l. Heart Verbs

In order to learn a language fast, you must learn many verbs for the actions you do with your legs!

为了快速学习一门语言，你必须学习许多动词，你用你的双腿做的动作！

¡Para aprender un idioma rápido, debes aprender muchos verbos para las acciones que haces con tus piernas!

언어를 빨리 배우려면 다리로하는 행동에 대한 동사를 많이 배워야합니다!

Chapter 16
How To Talk About How You Move
如何谈谈你移动腿部的不同方式
Cómo Hablar Sobre Cómo Te Mueves
당신이 어떻게 움직이는지를 표현하는 방법

Leg Verbs	Acquisition of New Vocabulary Directions in English: Write in Your Language Directions in Chinese: 用中文写 Directions in Spanish: Escribe En Tu Idioma Directions in Korea: 한글
1. Walk	
2. Run	
3. Jump	
4. Kick	
5. Stand	
6. Skip	
7. Hop	
8. Bend	
9. Cross	
10. Ride	

Leg Verbs

Directions in English: Write 3 times
Directions in Chinese: 写3次
Directions in Spanish: Escribe en Ingles
Directions in Korean: 영어로 3 번 쓰기

1. Walk	**Ex. Walk walk walk**
1. Walk	
2. Run	
3. Jump	
4. Kick	
5. Stand	
6. Skip	
7. Hop	
8. Bend	
9. Cross	
10. Ride	

Leg Verbs

GUESS THE VOCABULARY WORD
Directions in English: Guess the vocabulary word.
Directions in Chinese: 猜猜这个单词。
Directions in Spanish: Intenta descifrar la palabra del vocabulario.
Directions in Korean: 단어를 알아내시오.

1. klaw

2. nur

3. pmuj

4. kcik

5. dnats

6. piks

7. poh

8. dneb

9. ssorc

10. edir

LEG VERBS	I	YOU	HE/SHE/IT	WE	THEY
Walk	I walk	You walk	He or she walks	We walk	They walk
Walk					
Run					
Jump					
Kick					
Stand					
Skip					
Hop					
Bend					
Cross					
Ride					

16d. Whole Body Verbs – Conjugations - Find the appropriate verb写下合适的动词。 **Encuentra el verbo apropiado para el pronombre**대명사에 적절한 동사를 찾으십시오.

Leg Verbs	Directions in English: Underline The Verb Directions in Chinese: 强调动词。 Directions in Spanish: Subraya el verbo. Directions in Korean: 동사에 밑줄 치시오.
1. Walk	I walked to the store to buy a soda.
2. Run	Run before the dog catches you.
3. Jump	Jump over the fence quickly.
4. Kick	Kick the ball to your partner.
5. Stand	You should stand up if your name is called.
6. Skip	He skipped rope at the gym.
7. Hop	The rabbit hopped along slowly.
8. Bend	He bends his knees and raises up.
9. Cross	She crossed her legs during the meeting.
10. Ride	I ride the bus to work.

Leg Verbs

Directions in English: Copy The Sentence from the previous page
Directions in Chinese: 写下句子。
Directions in Spanish: Escribe la oracEón de la página anterior.
Directions in Korean: 이전 페이지에서 배운 문장을 다시 작성하시오.

1. Walk

2. Run

3. Jump

4. Kick

5. Stand

6. Skip

7. Hop

8. Bend

9. Cross

10. Ride

Leg Verbs

Directions in English: Fill In The Sentence
Directions in Chinese: 用模型句子中的正确单词填充句子。
Directions in Spanish: Completa la oración con las palabras correctas de las oraciones modelo.
Directions in Korean: 문장을 완성하시오.

1. Walk   I _____ to class.

2. Run   I _____ home.

3. Jump   I _____ out of bed.

4. Kick   I _____ the door.

5. Stand   I _____ up straight.

6. Skip   I _____ at the gym.

7. Hop   Rabbits like to _____.

8. Bend   I _____ my legs.

9. Cross   I _____ the street.

10. Ride   I _____ bikes.

Leg Verbs

Directions in English: Fill In The Sentence
Directions in Chinese: 用模型句子中的正确单词填充句子。
Directions in Spanish: Completa la oración con las palabras correctas de las oraciones modelo.
Directions in Korean: 문장을 완성하시오.

1. Walk   I walk _____ _____.

2. Run   I run _____.

3. Jump   I jump ___ __ ___.

4. Kick   I kick ___ _____.

5. Stand   I stand ___ _____.

6. Skip   I skip _____.

7. Hop   _____ like to hop.

8. Bend   I bend ___ _____.

9. Cross   I cross ___ _____.

10. Ride   I ride _____.

Leg Verbs	Directions in English: True / False。Put T or F Below Directions in Chinese: 在下面写正确或不正确 写T为正确或F 为不正确。 Directions in Spanish: Escribe T si es verdadero, F si es falso Directions in Korean: 참이면 T / 거짓이면 F 를 적으시오
1. Walk	I walked on the moon.
2. Run	Run before the sun catches you.
3. Jump	Jump over the rope.
4. Kick	Kick the ball into the window.
5. Stand	Stand up in the car.
6. Skip	Skip to the meeting.
7. Hop	Hop like a rabbit for the play.
8. Bend	Bend someone else's knees.
9. Cross	Look both ways before you cross the street.
10. Ride	We should ride our bikes to China.

Leg Verbs

Directions in English: Write a New Sentence with a dictionary.
Directions in Chinese: 写一个新的句子。
Directions in Spanish: Escribe una nueva oración creativa.
Directions in Korean: 새로운 창의적인 문장을 작성하시오.

1. Walk

2. Run

3. Jump

4. Kick

5. Stand

6. Skip

7. Hop

8. Bend

9. Cross

10. Ride

Leg Verbs

Directions in English: Questions - Translate to Your Language
Directions in Chinese: 用您的语言翻译
Directions in Spanish: Traducir en su idioma
Directions in Korean: 한국어로 번역하십시오.

1. Walk — Will you walk or take a bus?

2. Run — Where do you run?

3. Jump — Do you know how to jump rope?

4. Kick — Who kicked the ball over there?

5. Stand — How long did you stand?

6. Skip — Why do you skip over the cracks?

7. Hop — Where did it hop to?

8. Bend — Can you bend your knees?

9. Cross — Are you careful as you cross over?

10. Ride — Who can you get a ride with?

Leg Verbs

1. Walk

2. Run

3. Jump

4. Kick

5. Stand

6. Skip

7. Hop

8. Bend

9. Cross

10. Ride

Goodbyes	Directions in English: Write in your language and in English Directions in Chinese:用你的语言和英文写 Directions in Spanish:Escribe en tu idioma y en inglés Directions in Korean: 귀하의 언어와 영어로 작성하십시오.	
Bye!		
Bye Bye!		
See you later!		
Take care!		
See you soon!		
See you tomorrow!		
God bless!		

www.ingramcontent.com/pod-product-compliance
Lightning Source LLC
Chambersburg PA
CBHW081510040426
42447CB00013B/3174